AFRICAN
NAMES

RECLAIM YOUR HERITAGE

SAMAKI

Struik Publishers

(a division of New Holland Publishing (South Africa) (Pty) Ltd)

Cornelis Struik House

80 McKenzie Street

Cape Town 8001

South Africa

First Published in 2001

2 4 6 8 10 9 7 5 3 1

PUBLISHING MANAGER: Linda de Villiers

EDITOR: Cecilia Barfield

DESIGNER: Beverley Dodd

ARTWORK: Sharon Bernhardt

Cover reproduction by Hirt & Carter Cape (Pty) Ltd

ISBN 1 86872 685 1

I dedicate this book to my friend,

CREDO MUTWA

because without your inspiration and
encouragement this book would still be a dream.

ACKNOWLEDGEMENTS

I do not have words enough to thank Credo Mutwa – for his enthusiasm and for his encouragement. When I told him of my ideas he urged me to start work immediately. His knowledge is astounding. He has supported and assisted me with unfaltering confidence throughout the making of this book.

Doing the research became quite complicated at times and I would like to thank the following friends for their assistance and patience in helping me to source names and meanings.

Rose Khumalo
Rosinah Salome Mokgona
Agnes Sibongile Khubeka
Dorah Nkele Motebele
Lydia MatlakalaTlowana
Mapula Cathrina Ngyakomonye
Kabelo Mabalane
Steven Skwati Mahlangu
Adolphus Mandla Xulu
Kwanele Ngwenya

AUTHOR'S NOTE

When I was 12 years old my father was an engineer on a very remote tin mine in northwest Tanzania, near the border of Ruanda Burundi. He and the mine's geologist decided to make a boat trip up the Kagera River, which forms the border between Uganda and Tanzania, to take photographs of the wildlife in and alongside the river. I was invited to join them.

The river was in flood but they were confident that we could do it. We probably would have succeeded had the outboard motor not stalled causing us to be swept back downstream to our starting point where the ferry crossed the river. The ferry, one of those wonderfully primitive affairs with a steel cable running across the river, had somehow become hooked over the cable. A team of able-bodied young men normally pulled the ferry across by hauling the cable to the accompaniment of loud chanting and laughter.

On this fateful day, however, the ferry was out of service because of the flood and the steel cable was about a foot under the surface of the water. The small motorboat drifted down until it hit the cable and then capsized. My father and the geologist were thrown onto the cable but when I came up for air I was already a few meters away in the racing rapids of the flooding waters. I climbed up onto the bottom of the capsized boat just as the anchor caught some rocks on the riverbed. The boat completely disappeared under the water and left me in its swirling wake to swim frantically to the nearest and, needless to say, opposite bank.

I made it to the side amid cheers and applause from the audience, but it took a lot of money and much cajoling to persuade the ferrymen to bring the ferry across the raging

water to fetch me! From that day I was always known to the locals as 'Memsahib Samaki', samaki meaning fish. I later discovered that a family of crocodiles lived a few meters downstream and another family of hippos lived nearby, upstream.

It is for this reason that I have chosen to publish my book using my African name. Apart from being proud of it, I think it appropriate to use in this instance.

I have not divided the names into 'Girls' and 'Boys', mainly because some of the names are quite specific, such as, 'First Daughter' or 'Another Boy' and very often the names are unisex. Who am I to say that you may not call your daughter 'Bob' or 'James'? Ultimately, the choice is yours. But I hope you derive immense pleasure in choosing an appropriate name for your new baby.

SAMAKI

(Sharon J Bernhardt)

THE MAGIC IN THE NAME

'What's in a name?' That is the question posed by William Shakespeare in *Romeo and Juliet*. Among the people of Africa, a name is not regarded simply as a sound made into the empty air, a sound by which a thing or person is known and identified apart from others.

To us African people, your name is your soul. A name is an entity with a life of its own, apart from the life of the person who carries that name. According to the language of the Zulus and other Nguni-speaking people of South Africa, our word for name is *igama*. This word is very ancient and it literally means 'your symbol', because the original meaning of the word *igama* was a symbol engraved upon a flat stone. Long, long ago in Africa, when a child was named, the symbolic meaning of the child's name was painted on a round pebble in red or black pigment and this symbol was kept for as long as the person was alive. When that person died, the name-pebble was ritually broken into two pieces. With some tribes, again in those very ancient times, a person's name was incised with a sharp stone on a piece of hard wood, and when the person died, the carved symbol was ceremoniously burnt in a fire lit for the purpose.

The Batswana-, Northern Sotho- and Southern Sotho-speaking people have a most interesting word for a name – *leena*. The meaning of *leena* has to do with staying, remaining behind, immortality. That which stays behind after your death. African mysticism teaches us that when you name a child, you do not merely name the flesh and blood of that child (or the flesh and blood of a cow or goat or any other animal). The name is for the person's soul or the creature's soul.

A name is a thing so precious among our people that we believe very strongly that it possesses magical properties, which are bestowed upon you the moment you are named. Throughout your life you must ensure that your real name is protected against enemies as much as possible because we believe that if an enemy knows your name he can reverse that name and cause you great evil. For example, if your name happens to be Lesedi, which is Tswana or Sotho for 'light', an enemy will, if he wants to hurt you, reverse your name to Lefifi, which means 'darkness'. And so, even today, although Westernization has crept into almost every aspect of our lives, there are still people in South Africa who will not give you their real names until they know they can trust you absolutely. We find this amongst the Basuto people of Lesotho where a woman will marry a man and live with him for about ten years before she will trust him enough to tell him her real name.

I remember a woman I lived with in Lesotho. Her name was Mabalisa, a word that simply means 'mother of Balisa', who was her first-born child. I lived with this woman for a number of years before she trusted me enough to tell me that her real name was Pulane, which means 'daughter born in the rain', and not Mabalisa. When she told me her name, Pulane showed me that she now trusted me absolutely and loved me as deeply as one human being can love another.

Among our people, a person's name is so sacred that once the person has died, his or her name is never mentioned except by his or her closest relatives, and then only with the title before the name, which in Zulu is *umufi* which means 'the dead one' or in Tswana and Sotho, *muswi*. For instance, if a person's name is Nko, which means 'nose', after death

the person will be known as *muswiNko*, which means 'the dead one named Nko', and when you say the word *muswiNko*, you must put a very soft accent upon the dead person's name. Some people never mention a dead person at all except by referring to the dead one who died on a particular day and in a particular year. In times past, our people took great care not to give children names with negative meanings because they believed, and quite rightly, that a person's name follows the person and dictates the fate of their life.

Now what do I mean by that? Take heed of the following story. There was once in the land of the Zulus, a king named Shaka. The name Shaka means 'a stomach complaint where the victim's stomach swells up', in other words, dropsy. Dropsy is a very tormenting illness indeed and the man called Shaka did torment many nations. He lived out his name. Shaka had a half brother called Dingane. The name Dingane means 'exiled', or 'the little exile'. It derives from the verb *dinga* that means 'to expel, to exile, the exiling of a person'. Now King Dingane murdered Shaka, his brother, and took over the kingship of the Zulus. He ruled for about eight years before he was overthrown by an alliance of Zulus (his own people) and Voortrekkers. Dingane, after the terrible battle of Magogo was forced into exile in the land of the Mangwane people, where he was captured by an old enemy. For a number of days, this enemy slowly tortured Dingane to death. Dingane, the little exile, did indeed die in exile.

Now, let me show you further. The chaos in Zululand that followed the overthrow and death of Dingane was brought to an end by the coming of Mpande, another half brother of Shaka. Mpande brought stability and peace into the land of the Zulus for a very long time. His was a peaceful reign at a

very dangerous time when white settlers were moving into Natal in large numbers. Mpande did everything in his power to ensure peace in the land of the Zulus. Do you know what the name Mpande means? It means 'tap root'. It means 'the great root of a tree' and nothing holds a tree more firmly to the ground than its roots. King 'Root' Mpande became a symbol of peace at a time when the Zulu nation was being shaken to its foundations. But wait, there is more to this amazing story.

King Mpande had a number of sons who started fighting for kingship while Mpande was still alive. And among these sons was Cetshwayo, who became king of the Zulus. During his reign Zululand was torn by wars from one end to the other. Under Cetshwayo the terrible battles of Isandlwane and Ulundi were fought. After the battle of Ulundi, King Cetshwayo fled into the Nkandla forest and was in hiding for some time. But Zulu traitors went to the British army, which was camped in many parts of Zululand, and revealed Cetshwayo's exact hiding place. The British sent a powerful force of soldiers into the Nkandla forest to apprehend the betrayed Zulu king. Now, what does that have to do with names? Well, the name Cetshwayo means 'the one who has been informed upon or the betrayed one' and King Cetshwayo was betrayed precisely according to the meaning of his name.

The story continues. After King Cetshwayo, there came to the Zulu throne a tragic king, whose name was Dinizulu. What a remarkable name. The name Dinizulu means 'the one who satisfies the Zulus'. And like his name, although he was brutally harassed by the British, and was tortured, jailed and humiliated for crimes he had not committed, King Dinizulu did everything he possibly could to keep the land of the Zulus peaceful and stable. He became great friends with Bishop Colenso and his two daughters. King Dinizulu gave his people peace, even though he received none at the hands of the British – his deadliest and most obsessive enemies. During the terrible war known as the Zulu Rebellion of 1906, King Dinizulu was unjustly imprisoned by the British and brutally tortured because he was accused of having sheltered the wives of King Bambata, the leader of the Zulu rebellion. But in spite of all that, Dinizulu, the peacemaker, the one who satisfies the Zulus, remained true to his name. Sometimes, in his pursuit of peace, Dinizulu made mistakes for which his people later condemned him. All because he was a man who believed in peace – peace at any price.

The power of the name is still as important in modern Africa as it was in ancient times, and often we see evidence of this in what some of Africa's greatest and most successful leaders have done over the years. In the Africa of old, if you wanted to acquire spiritual power you had to change your name and be given, or give yourself, a new one. This symbolized rebirth in Africa no matter where, despite the vastness of the Dark Continent. Let me explain.

There was once a man in East Africa (born c 1891), who was falsely accused of being a leader of a bloody, black rebellion and who was jailed for crimes he did not commit and could not possibly have committed. This man had a very insignificant and rather ridiculous name. It was Stanley Kamau. But the wings of fate propelled Stanley Kamau into a position of leadership over one of the great nations in East Africa. After a spell in prison, Stanley Kamau found himself elected leader of the nation of Kenya. Just as Great Britain was preparing to grant that nation independence, Stanley Kamau must have realized that he had inherited trouble, because, as you know, Kenya is inhabited by some of the fiercest warrior tribes in all Africa. In Kenya you find the warrior Masai, a nation with a warlike tradition that goes back hundreds, if not thousands, of years. Also in Kenya are the warrior Wakamba, the Turkana, the Kiisii, the Gikuyu and other great tribes whose history goes back hundreds of years. Kamau knew that he had to do something because he was venturing forth into a political, as well as a tribal mine-field. What was he to do?

Stanley Kamau changed his name. He called himself, Jomo Kenyatta. Jomo means 'burning spear' – a spear which is heated till it is red-hot and thrown over the stockade at enemy huts to set them alight. Kenyatta was a dramatic name. A play on words – a kenyatta was a type of beaded belt which was in fashion throughout East Africa at that time and Stanley Kamau named himself after this. Thus Jomo Kenyatta emerged from Stanley Kamau. In this great act of self-baptism Jomo Kenyatta was easily able to rule a nation, which was indeed extremely volatile. Moreover, he placed himself above all tribal divisions and disputes by adopting the title Mzee, which means 'wise old man, the one who has the knowledge'. He was to rule as the Mzee for many, many years and he ruled a large, peaceful and prosperous nation. When Jomo Kenyatta died his successor, Daniel Arap Moi, chose the path of continuity. He told the people that he was Jomo Kenyatta's Initiate and Successor, and whereas Jomo Kenyatta had carried the ceremonial fly whisk, Arap Moi carried the type of walking stick that a High Initiate, walking in the footsteps of a great teacher, would carry.

Now, let us go to another part of Africa where something similar occurred, but this time, much earlier. There was once a man whose original name I have forgotten, but this man changed his name twice. First there was his original name, then he changed that and became known as Kwame Nkrumah, the West African leader of the first country in Africa to be given independence, if one can call it that, from Britain. Kwame Nkrumah ruled his people's country, Ghana, peacefully for some years and then, at some point added a name, or rather, a title to his name. The title was Osegyefo, which means 'savior of the people'.

But before I go any further, let us turn back again, this time to Tanganyika, or as it is now known, Tanzania – where for many years a black intellectual held sway, a man who saw himself as the great teacher of Africa. Julius Nyerere, Julius, the Quiet, was the man's name and, because in Africa every leader must have a baptism and a ritual change of name, Julius Nyerere gave himself a title – Mwalumi, a word which means 'the great teacher'. Until he stepped down as leader, Julius Nyerere was known as Mwalumi Julius Nyerere, the teacher of Africa.

But now, in a very long list, let me tell you about one last man. In the troubled years of the 1960s, after bloody battles had torn the former Belgian Congo from north to south and east to west, there arose an insignificant little corporal, whose name was Joseph Mobutu.

What power did Mobutu possess that he was able to bring peace to the Congo. Something that had defeated the efforts of the United Nations and all its blue-helmeted thugs. The name Mobutu has a very deep, magical meaning in many parts of Africa. It is one of the oldest names in our history.

And if you really want to understand Africa, I will give you a quest to follow. Find out for yourself the meaning of the name Mobutu. I won't tell you. You find out. Mobutu, like Jomo Kenyatta in Kenya, found himself riding what could possibly become a dangerous beast. A huge, scaly monster comprising many violent, and some of the most untamed, tribes anywhere in Africa. The country once known as the Belgian Congo is even larger than South Africa and consists of many, many black tribes and nations. In it you will find people who stand almost seven feet tall, as well as people who stand just a mere four feet high – the pygmies (one of the oldest races on earth).

How was Mobutu going to rule this explosive nation? This nation which had defeated the efforts of great men like Patrice Lumumba, Moysa Chombe and Kasa Vuba, to name but three. Firstly, he gathered around himself a group, a powerful force of female warriors, just as the God of Light in African mythology is said to be surrounded by. These were his parabats, his parachute soldiers, whom the Belgians contemptuously referred to as Les Paramours. The world laughed at Joseph Mobutu, but this African knew what he was doing and he ruled the country, which he named Zaire, for a long, long time, until he died of cancer a few years ago. Like Jomo Kenyatta, Joseph Mobutu went through the ritual of self-baptism and named himself Mobutu Seseseku Kuku Sangbetu. A long name which simply means, 'Mobutu, the Black Rooster which deflowers all the hens in the village'. It sounded rather bombastic, but it earned the respect of many African people.

I could go on and on. He was originally called Hastings Banda, but when his long rule came to an end he was

no longer known as Hastings Banda but Ngwasi Kamuzu Banda. There is another name. A name, which goes back hundreds of years. A name whose meaning is 'the armed attacker', Mugabe. The original meaning of Mugabe is 'weaponed attacker'. A warrior's name. What hasn't Mugabe done to live up to his name? Many a white farmer knows, to his cost.

There is a great man in South Africa. A man with a beautiful and remarkable name. A name, which, out of respect, I cannot divulge the meaning of. But this great man's name is Rolihlahla. The world knows him as Nelson Mandela, but one of his names is Rolihlahla. Rola has to do with leadership, with leading something or pushing something out of the way so that people may pass. What is that something? This great man, as the leader of the ANC, as the leader of the nation of South Africa, and today as the leader of a mission seeking to promote peace on the troubled continent of Africa, has more than lived up to his name. Nelson Mandela is a man of royal blood and, as such, I am honor-bound to show respect to his name, Rolihlahla. You, gentle reader, must find out for yourself, exactly, what the name Rolihlahla means and it will be an enlightening experience for you.

In Africa the power of the name is still as revered as it was in ancient times. When an African child is named, he or she is often given as many as 20 names. He or she is given his or her real name, which is protected by a layer of other names. Sometimes in a community, you will find members of a family calling a member of that family by a number of different names because when a child is born each elderly relative gives the child a particular name by which that relative insists on knowing the child to the end of his or her days.

I am named Credo Mpumelelo Mutwa. My real name, the name that my mother gave me, is Vusamazulu – that is the name I only tell my friends. The rest must be content with Credo Mpumelelo. But I have another name – a female name that was given to me by my mother, who had greatly wished to be given a female child by the gods. That name is Mankanyesi which means 'female child of many stars', but with the grey beard that I am now beginning to sport, I don't look very female, do I?

But sometimes an African parent will give his or her child a name actually belonging to the opposite sex. There was once a great warrior in Zululand, the bravest man who ever lived. This man lived in the time of the Zulu King, Dingane, and he was truly a hero of heroes. But what was this man's name? His name was Nozishada. The name Nozishada is really a girl's name, but because Nozishada's father had wanted a daughter, he had named his son by the name Nozishada.

Whenever you name a child, you must be fully aware of the exact meaning of that child's name because it seems that when someone is named, a certain energy in the universe is activated – an energy which shall follow that name.

Africa is a remarkable continent, a mysterious land, and the more I live within its borders, the more surprised I am by the ways of my people and the strange forces that African magic is still able to bring into play, even in this electronic age. There is a phrase in Latin, *Nomen est Omen* – 'your name is your omen'. This is true, it was always true and it will always be true. A name is magic. A name is something that remains after you are gone. If William Shakespeare had not had his strange and remarkable name, would we have remembered him? The answer is 'No!' Would we have remembered

George Washington if he had not had a name? The answer is 'No.' I sometimes ask myself – is the, supposedly immortal, human soul actually the name by which that person was named at birth? Are names our passport to immortality? I do not know, and I do not want to know. But I want to end this introduction with a strange Zulu song, which Zulus used to sing when they went into battle knowing that they might not come back alive.

Noma ngingafa -
Ikhona indodana!
Negama lami likhona!

Refrain: Gama lami ye Ma
Noma ngingafa likhona
Gama lami ye Ma
Igama lami likhona!

Translated, this means 'Even if I die in the coming battle, my son is there and my name is also there.'

Again..... what's in a name? Thanks, thank you to everyone.

CREDO VUSAMAZULU MUTWA

PHONETICS

As a general rule most African languages are spoken very phonetically, however it can be quite awkward for Westerners to get their tongues around some of the letters. For example, Qs, Cs and Xs in many languages are sounded as 'clicks' and 'tuts'. I have not dwelt on these letters in depth, but obviously they cannot be omitted altogether. Without going into linguistics in great detail, the following is a very simple guide to help with pronunciations.

A – as in father, sofa. or about
E – as in pet or eh
I – as ee in feet
O – is used to represent two sounds as in shawl and coat
U – as in fool

Where there are two or three letters together, such as ai, au, ua or aoa, each letter is pronounced as above (aaee, aaoo, ooaa or aaoaa).

Y is pronounced as the English word yeast.
W is pronounced as the English word well.
B, D, G, K, P and T are pronounced softly without aspiration, e.g. bat, dog, goat, keep, put and tap. Never pronounce G as in George!
BH, PH, TH, KH are pronounced as above, only stronger – not as in phone or this.
F, V, R, M, N, L are pronounced almost the same as in English, although the R should be rolled more.
NG represents the sound as in singing when 'in' precedes a

vowel. But before K or G the sound is represented by plain 'n'.

S is pronounced as in <u>s</u>ing and never as in ro<u>s</u>e.

Z is pronounced as in <u>z</u>eal or the S in ro<u>s</u>e.

TS is pronounced as in si<u>ts</u>.

TSH is pronounced like ch in <u>ch</u>urch or tch in wa<u>tch</u>.

J, SH, D are pronounced as they are in English.

DL is a merging of the normal English D and L sounds.

HL is pronounced like the Welsh LL.

TY, DY and NY are heard in <u>t</u>une, <u>d</u>ue and <u>n</u>ew.

CLICKS

The clicks, represented by C, Q, and X are suction sounds, produced by creating a vacuum between the tongue and the palate, and suddenly withdrawing the tongue, thus allowing an inrush of air.

For C, the tip of the tongue is placed against the top of the upper front teeth and it is the sound sometimes made in English to express exasperation, a 'tut'.

For Q the tongue is placed between the teeth ridge and the hard palate.

For X the tongue is placed as for Q, but the withdrawal takes place at the side instead of in the front of the mouth.

CH, QH and XH all represent aspirated varieties of the simple clicks.

NC, NQ and NX represent nasalized clicks.

GC, GQ and GX are the simple voiced forms of the clicks.

NGC, NGQ and NGX are nasalized forms, accompanied by voiced glottal friction.

As you can see, some of the click sounds need a lot of practice and may be difficult for most people to pronounce, unless it's your native language. However, for example, many people in South Africa pronounce Xhosa as 'corza' because of the difficulty in using the correct clicking pronunciation. Although, strictly speaking, this is incorrect, it is done.

SHARON J BERNHARDT

AMBANI - ANTBEAR

AADIL	Honorable, fair-minded	ARABIC
AAILYAH	Of the highest order	SWAHILI
AASIM	Benefactor, champion	ARABIC
ABA	Thursday	NGUNI
ABA	To share out	ZULU
ABABUO	Child that has come back	NGUNI
ABADI	Everlasting blessing	ARABIC
ABEBI	Asked for girl child	W AFRICAN
ABELO	Free gift	ZULU
ABEO	I bring joy	W AFRICAN
ABIDEMI	Girl child born during her father's absence	NGUNI
ABIRIA	Passenger	SWAHILI
ABLA	Wild rose	SWAHILI
ABONA	The best	TSONGA
ADA	Oldest daughter	W AFRICAN
ADAEZE	Princess	W AFRICAN
ADAMA	Awesome, magnificent child	W AFRICAN
ADANNE	Daughter that resembles her mother	W AFRICAN

ADE	The pinnacle, peak	W AFRICAN
ADERO	She who creates life	C AFRICAN
ADWIN	Creative, imaginative	W AFRICAN
AFAFA	First daughter of second husband	W AFRICAN
AFIFA	Spiritual, holy	W AFRICAN
AFLA	Health	SWAHILI
AFUA	Mercy	SWAHILI
AHADI	Promise	SWAHILI
AHSAN	Gentle and understanding	ARABIC
AIDOO	Achieve recognition	W AFRICAN
AJABU	Wonder, astonishment	SWAHILI
AJALA	Believer of Allah	W AFRICAN
AJALI	Destiny, fate	SWAHILI
AKHONA	They are present	ZULU
AKIDA	Officer, captain	SWAHILI
AKILI	Wisdom, sense	SWAHILI
AKO	The first son	W AFRICAN
AKRAM	Open-handed, big-hearted	ARABIC
ALAMA	Sign, token	SWAHILI
ALAMISI	Thursday	SWAHILI
ALASIRI	Afternoon	SWAHILI
ALFAJIRI	Dawn	SWAHILI
ALILI	She who complains	W AFRICAN
ALUKI	Basket weaver	ZULU
ALUSA	To watch over, to tend	ZULU
ALUSI	Shepherd, cowherd	ZULU
AMA	Daughter born on Saturday	W AFRICAN
AMA	Happy and joyful son	W AFRICAN
AMALI	Endeavor, hope	SWAHILI
AMANA	Trust	SWAHILI
AMANI	Peace, harmony	SWAHILI

AMBALO	Jewel	TSONGA
AMBANI	Antbear	NGUNI
AMBATA	Embrace	SWAHILI
AMBE	We begged God for this child	W AFRICAN
AMBOMBO	Heavy rain	ZULU
AMEEN	Loyal and true	ARABIC
AMEER	Monarch, prince	ARABIC
AMIR	Leader, prince	ARABIC
AMIRA	Princess	SWAHILI
AMIRI	Prince	SWAHILI
AMKELA	Receive	TSONGA
AMNE	Secure	SWAHILI
AMRI	Power	SWAHILI
AMWA	To be suckled	SWAHILI
ANABE	One held in honor	TSONGA
ANAN	Fourth-born child	W AFRICAN
ANANA	Exchange	TSONGA
ANAPA	Child born at daybreak	W AFRICAN
ANDAIYE	A daughter comes home	SWAHILI
ANDI	Loud noise	XHOSA
ANDILE	More children	XHOSA
ANDLE	Sea, ocean	ZULU
ANELA	Be satisfied	ZULU
ANELE	Enough children	XHOSA
ANELISA	To satisfy	ZULU
ANGA	Air, atmosphere	SWAHILI
ANGALIA	To observe, to watch	SWAHILI
ANGAZA	To keep ones eyes open	SWAHILI
ANISA	Friendly	SWAHILI
ANISHA	The day star	XHOSA
ANTWAR	Moonbeams, sunbeams	ARABIC

ANULI	Daughter who brings happiness	W AFRICAN
ANZA	Beginning	SWAHILI
ARAFAT	Mount of recognition	ARABIC
ARAZAKI	Provider	SWAHILI
ARUBAA	Fourth-born	SWAHILI
ASALI	Nectar, honey	SWAHILI
ASANI	Rebellious	SWAHILI
ASANTE	Thank you	SWAHILI
ASHIA	Meaningful existence	E AFRICAN
ASHRAF	Righteous, virtuous	ARABIC
ASIF	Mercy	ARABIC
ASILI	Original	SWAHILI
ASIYA	Console, pacify	SWAHILI
ASUBUHI	Morning	SWAHILI
ASYA	Brilliant	E AFRICAN
ATIFAR	Understanding, kindness	ARABIC
ATILE	Increasing family	SOTHO
ATO	This one is brilliant	SWAHILI
AUNI	To help, succor	SWAHILI
AVA	To divide	TSONGA
AVU	Dove	XHOSA
AWAD	Prize, honor	ARABIC
AWENA	Gentle	SWAHILI
AYAH	Sparkling, twinkling	W AFRICAN
AYAMA	Someone to lean on	XHOSA
AYAN	Brilliant	E AFRICAN
AYANDA	Another one	ZULU
AYANNA	Beautiful blossom	E AFRICAN
AYELE	Powerful man	E AFRICAN
AYISI	Ice	TSONGA
AYIZE	Let it come	ZULU

AYO	Joyful	W AFRICAN
AZA	Powerful, strong	SWAHILI
AZIMA	Resolve, determination	SWAHILI
AZISA	Honor, esteem, pride	ZULU
AZIZ	Precious	SWAHILI
AZIZA	Exquisite child	E AFRICAN
AZIZI	Adored and cherished child	SWAHILI

B

BABALA - BUSHBUCK

BABALA	Bushbuck	NGUNI
BABALA	Favor, grace	XHOSA
BABALLA	To take care of	S SOTHO
BABATU	Mediator, he who brings peace	W AFRICAN
BABAVANA	Tall and slender person	ZULU
BABU	A healer	E AFRICAN
BABU	Ancestor	SWAHILI
BADIMO	Ancestral spirits	N SOTHO
BADO	Not yet, wait awhile	SWAHILI
BADU	Tenth child	W AFRICAN
BAFANA	Boys	ZULU
BAHARI	Sea, large lake	SWAHILI
BAHATI	Luck, fortune	SWAHILI
BAHATI	Good fortune	W AFRICAN
BAINA	Bright, glittering, sparkling	W AFRICAN
BAKABAKA	Pretty woman	ZULU
BAKALLA	Restorer of virility	S SOTHO
BAKISHISHI	Gift	SWAHILI
BALA	To tell a story, to read a story	NGUNI

BALARA	Champion	XHOSA
BALEKA	A fast runner	XHOSA
BALELA	Clear skies	ZULU
BALI	Contrary	SWAHILI
BALISA	A flower	SOTHO
BALIWE	Rejected	ZULU
BALOZI	Consul, commissioner	SWAHILI
BALULA	To choose	XHOSA
BAMBA	Counsel	SWAHILI
BAMBATA	Great warrior who led rebellion	XHOSA
BAMBELI	Substitute	ZULU
BANDA	Birthmark, scar	XHOSA
BANDA	Very clever person	ZULU
BANDILE	They have grown	ZULU
BANE	Candle, light	XHOSA
BANI	Flash of lightning	ZULU
BARAKA	Prosperity, mystical blessings	SWAHILI
BASA	Clean, pure, bright	TSONGA
BASELA	Gift, small present	TSONGA
BASHA	Act of God	SWAHILI
BASI	Enough, that will do!	SWAHILI
BASIMANEGAPE	More boys	N SOTHO
BASMA	Smile	SWAHILI
BATHA	Spider's web	XHOSA
BAWA	Greedy, voracious	XHOSA
BAWO	Benefactor, master	XHOSA
BAYO	Great joy is found	W AFRICAN
BEBEZA	To tell fairy tales	XHOSA
BEHLALE	Wise	N SOTHO
BEJIDE	Child born during the rains	W AFRICAN
BEKA	Honor, respect	XHOSA

BEKA-PANSI	The observant one who looks on the ground	NGUNI
BEKEBEKE	Glittering, shining	ZULU
BELA	To burst forth, to bubble up	SOTHO
BENYA	To be bright, to shine	S SOTHO
BENYA-KGANYA	Shimmering light	SOTHO
BETA	Little child crying	S SOTHO
BETOTO	Owl	SWAHILI
BEYAKANYA	People who shine	SOTHO
BHABHA	Struggle for freedom	XHOSA
BHADI	Springbuck, butterfly	XHOSA
BHADULA	To wander, roam about	XHOSA
BHEDU	Copper	XHOSA
BHEKI	Watchman, caretaker	ZULU
BHELU	A very handsome person	XHOSA
BHUTI	Brother	XHOSA
BIASHARA	Trade	SWAHILI
BIBI	Lady, mistress	SWAHILI
BIKA	Announcement, omen	SOTHO
BILASHI	For nothing, free	SWAHILI
BIN	Son	SWAHILI
BINA	To sing, to dance	S SOTHO
BINADAMU	Son of Adam	SWAHILI
BINI	A pair	XHOSA
BINTI	Daughter of a beautiful son	SWAHILI
BINZA	An expert spearman	XHOSA
BISI	Sweet milk, brandy	XHOSA
BIZA	Invitation	XHOSA
BODIBA	Deep place, valley	N SOTHO
BODWA	Alone, only	XHOSA
BOFEJANE	Youngest child, the last one	N SOTHO

BOFELO	Destiny, fate	N SOTHO
BOFULA	Struggle	XHOSA
BOFUMO	Wealth, riches	S SOTHO
BOGALE	Sharp as a knife, fierce	N SOTHO
BOHLALE	A clever and intelligent child	N SOTHO
BOHLOKWA	Special	N SOTHO
BOITEKANELO	Health	N SOTHO
BOITSHEPEGI	Trustworthy, faithful	N SOTHO
BOITSHEPI	Self-confident	N SOTHO
BOKAONE	Better	N SOTHO
BOLADE	Honor comes with this child, honor arrives	W AFRICAN
BOMBA	Pretty	TSONGA
BOMBO	Mountains	ZULU
BOMBU	Brown, red	XHOSA
BONANI	To take care of, to guard	NGUNI
BONDE	Valley	SWAHILI
BONGA	Praise, poetry, a lullaby	XHOSA
BONGANE	Thanks	NGUNI
BONGANI	Sing with joy, be thankful	NGUNI
BONGINKOSI	Thank the Lord	ZULU
BONGIWE	Asked for girl child, we are grateful	ZULU
BONGUMUSA	Thanks for His mercy	ZULU
BONISWA	This has been revealed	NGUNI
BONOLO	Easy	N SOTHO
BONTLE	Gorgeous child, beautiful and bright	N SOTHO
BOPHELO	Life	N SOTHO
BOPO	Deep place, valley	SWAHILI
BORA	Noble, great, important	SWAHILI
BOSIGO	Night	N SOTHO

BOTHO	Humane person	SOTHO
BOTLOKWA	Noble, great, very important	SOTHO
BOTSANA	The best	SOTHO
BOTSE	Pretty woman	SOTHO
BUBUJIKA	To bubble up, to burst forth	SWAHILI
BUBULUNDU	Fat child of the royal kraal	ZULU
BUHLE	Beautiful	XHOSA
BUIBUI	Spider	SWAHILI
BUKUTHU	Plump child	ZULU
BULELANI	Let us be thankful	XHOSA
BUMBANA	Unity, to hold together	ZULU
BUNGE	Good luck, popularity	ZULU
BURUJI	Castle, fortress	SWAHILI
BUSA	To return something, bring it back	SOTHO
BUSARA	Prudence, sense, understanding, wisdom	SWAHILI
BUSI	Ruler, governor	ZULU
BUSISIWE	Blessed	NGUNI
BUSISO	Blessing, benediction	ZULU
BUSU	Kiss	SWAHILI
BUTSISA	To ask questions repeatedly	SOTHO
BUTU	Sleepy, tired	W AFRICAN
BUYA	To return	XHOSA
BUYANG	Child that returns	SOTHO
BUYANI	Come back to us	ZULU
BUYISANA	Reconciled	ZULU
BUYISILE	The one who has come back	NGUNI
BUYU	Calabash	SWAHILI
BUZA	To ask questions	ZULU
BYANI	Come back	ZULU

CELANKOBE
EVENING STAR

CACA	Plainly seen or heard	XHOSA
CAKAZA	To scatter	ZULU
CAMANGA	Think, meditate	XHOSA
CAMARA	She passes on her knowledge	W AFRICAN
CANZIBE	Bright star, Canopus seen before daybreak in May	XHOSA
CARAZA	Rustle, crackle	XHOSA
CATHULA	Toddling, learning to walk	ZULU
CAWEKAZI	Woman of the day of worship	NGUNI
CAZA	To portion out, share	ZULU
CEBA	Advisor, counselor	XHOSA
CEBO	Riches, wealth	ZULU
CELA	Immortal	ZULU
CELANI	Ask	NGUNI
CELANKOBE	Evening star	ZULU
CELUMUSA	Ask for mercy	ZULU
CETHULA	Clear sky	ZULU
CETSHWAYO	The betrayed one	ZULU
CHABASA	Walk slowly, tread softly	XHOSA
CHACHA	Sleek	ZULU

CHACHAMBA	In good condition	XHOSA
CHACHAZO	Stream, brook	ZULU
CHAKIJANE	Cunning fellow, mongoose	ZULU
CHAMBA	Shelter, haven	SWAHILI
CHANA	A good shot, marksman	XHOSA
CHANTI	Water spirit	XHOSA
CHAPHA	Touched with the first rays of the sun	XHOSA
CHASA	An opponent	XHOSA
CHASI	To be alert, watchful	XHOSA
CHAUSIKU	Born after the sunset	SWAHILI
CHAVEKA	To be honored, feared	TSONGA
CHAVELELA	Calm, console, comfort	TSONGA
CHEBE	Chance, luck, fortune	XHOSA
CHEFE	Softness, tenderness	ZULU
CHEMBE	Arrowhead	SWAHILI
CHENZA	Orange, tangerine	SWAHILI
CHEZA	To dance	SWAHILI
CHEZU	Branching off	ZULU
CHIBI	Pond, pool	XHOSA
CHIKU	Talks incessantly, chatterbox	C AFRICAN
CHINUE	Blessing from God	C AFRICAN
CHIPHIZA	Shed tears	ZULU
CHIPO	Gift	ZULU
CHOBOKA	Frail, delicate person	ZULU
CHOCHOYI	Mountain top, pinnacle	XHOSA
CHOKA	Polite, refined	XHOSA
CHOTHO	Hail	ZULU
CHUKUSA	Meticulous	XHOSA
CHULUMACHA	Self-confident	XHOSA
CHUMA	God understands	W AFRICAN

CHUMA	Flourish, be fruitful, prosper	XHOSA
CHUNXA	Liberate	TSONGA
CHWAMA	Bushman	XHOSA
CHWAYA	Noisy, sing loudly	ZULU
CHWAYITA	Rejoice loudly, happy, joyful	XHOSA
CHWEBA	Lake, lagoon, harbor, haven	ZULU
CIBISHOLO	Arrow	ZULU
CICANE	The little toe	XHOSA
CIINGELA	To look behind	TSONGA
CIKEKA	Satisfied	ZULU
CIKI	Fullness	ZULU
CIKICANE	The little finger	XHOSA
CIKO	Fluent, eloquent speaker	XHOSA
CIKO	Gifted person, dancer or singer	ZULU
CILONGA	Trumpet	ZULU
CIMILA	Soften	TSONGA
CINELELA	Persistence	ZULU
CINGA	A stalk of grass, anything thin	XHOSA
CINGA	To search for	ZULU
COCA	Cleansed, purified	XHOSA
COLOTHI	Twilight, dusk	XHOSA
COMBELA	To do one's best	XHOSA
COPETA	Twinkle	TSONGA
CWALA	Sit and wait	XHOSA
CWATHA	Cloudless	ZULU
CWAZIMULA	Shine brightly	ZULU

DANGALA - BABOON

DABA	Report, message	XHOSA
DABAZO	Rushing away, running off	XHOSA
DABU	Origin	ZULU
DABUKO	Traditional custom, origin	ZULU
DABULAMANZI	Crosses the waters	ZULU
DADA	Child with curly hair	W AFRICAN
DADA	Float, swim	XHOSA
DADE	Sister	ZULU
DAEMANE	Diamond	S SOTHO
DAIB	Outstanding daughter	E AFRICAN
DAKARAI	Child brings joy, happiness	W AFRICAN
DAKASA	Ramble, rove	XHOSA
DALA	Create, something new	XHOSA
DALI	The Creator	ZULU
DALILA	Gentle girl, gentleness is her soul	W AFRICAN
DALILI	A token or sign	W AFRICAN
DAMBA	To become calm	XHOSA
DAMU	Sudden relief	ZULU
DANDALAZA	Come into the open	ZULU
DANDALAZISA	Make prominent, clear	XHOSA

DANDALUKA	Call or cry out loud	XHOSA
DANGALA	Baboon	ZULU
DANGALA	Languid, listless	XHOSA
DANGAZELA	Intense desire	XHOSA
DANSA	Dance	ZULU
DAVATHI	Anklet of beads	ZULU
DAYO	We have found joy, joy has arrived	W AFRICAN
DAZA	Obstinate, persistent	ZULU
DAZULUKA	Shout loudly, scream	ZULU
DEDELA	To release or let go	XHOSA
DEDELANA	Make way for each other	XHOSA
DEKA	She who satisfies	XHOSA
DELANI	I am content now	ZULU
DEMBEZA	Stately, dignified	XHOSA
DENE	Water lily	W AFRICAN
DHARUBA	Storm	XHOSA
DIA	The winner, the best	W AFRICAN
DIARRA	Blessing, offering	W AFRICAN
DIBA	Fountain, spring	TSONGA
DIBANA	Mix together, mingle together	ZULU
DIDA	Puzzle, mystery, riddle	ZULU
DIDIMA	Multitude	TSONGA
DIDIZA	Flutter, tingle, tremble	ZULU
DIKELA	Setting of the sun	TSONGA
DIKELEDI	A child who was born during sorrow	SOTHO
DIKIDA	Tickle	TSONGA
DIKIWE	More than satisfied	W AFRICAN
DILIZA	Destroyer of evil	SWAHILI
DIMAKATSO	Wonder, astonishment	N SOTHO

DIMAKATSO	A child who makes wonders	NGUNI
DIMAKATSO	Many miracles	SOTHO
DINEO	Gift	NGUNI
DINGA	To wander, to be without a home	ZULU
DINGANE	Exiled, the little exile	ZULU
DINIZULU	The one who satisfies the Zulus	ZULU
DINO	An expert spearman, celebration	SOTHO
DISA	To watch over, to tend	TSONGA
DITHABA	Mountains	N SOTHO
DLULAMITHI	Giraffe (above the trees)	ZULU
DOBOLWANE	Friend	XHOSA
DODA	Man, male, husband	ZULU
DODAKAZI	Daughter	ZULU
DODANA	Son	ZULU
DOGO	Little	SWAHILI
DOKOZA	To speak with a deep, gruff voice	XHOSA
DOKOZELA	To speak with a deep, gruff voice	XHOSA
DOLO	Great multitude, abundance	XHOSA
DOLOMBA	Wave or undulate	XHOSA
DOMBOZA	Thank flatteringly	XHOSA
DONDO	The chief man of a place	XHOSA
DONDOSHIYA	Tall, muscular person	ZULU
DONDOTHA	To repeat exactly	XHOSA
DONYA	Star, white spot on face of animal	ZULU
DOSHABA	Deep voice	ZULU
DUDU	Insect	SWAHILI
DUDUMA	Thunder, rumble	XHOSA
DUDUZA	Comfort	ZULU
DUDUZILE	We have been comforted	ZULU
DUELELE	Big, strong person	TSONGA
DUKUDUKU	Whirlwind, tornado	TSONGA

DULU	Highly priced, expensive	XHOSA
DULUSA	Favorite, to stand out	XHOSA
DUMA	Shout of triumph	XHOSA
DUMA	Famous, well known	ZULU
DUMA	Lightning, thunder	ZULU
DUMELA	To be joyful, to believe, have faith	TSONGA
DUMEZULU	Something big and exciting	ZULU
DUMISA	Praise, worship	ZULU
DUMO	Fame, renown	ZULU
DUNDU	Reaching the top	ZULU
DUNDUBALA	Reach the top, climax	ZULU
DUNDUZELA	To lull to sleep	ZULU
DUNGA – MALE	To fly away, scatter, disperse	XHOSA
DUNGU – FEMALE	To fly away, scatter, disperse	XHOSA
DUNGUDELA	Vagabond, wanderer	XHOSA
DUNGULU	Black wasp	XHOSA
DUNKUNKA	A mystery	XHOSA
DUNYELWA	Famous or renowned person	XHOSA
DUPA	To divine, to procure by magic	TSONGA
DUTSWANE	Hunt undertaken to bring rain	TSONGA
DUTUVA	Overcast, cloudy	TSONGA
DWANGUBE	A chief counselor	XHOSA
DYAMBU	Day, sunlight	TSONGA
DYEBO	Great harvest, abundance of food	XHOSA
DYESHA	A well-built youth	XHOSA
DYOLI	Secret messenger	XHOSA
DZANGA	Reserved, shy, silent	TSONGA
DZELIWE	We are satisfied	SWAZI
DZINDZA	Thunder	TSONGA
DZONGA	South	TSONGA
DZUNISA	Praise, glory	TSONGA

EBU - SPIDER'S WEB

EBERE	Charity, kindness	W AFRICAN
EBU	Spider's web	NGUNI
EFIA	Friday's child, born on Friday	W AFRICAN
EJAJA	Be jovial, merry	ZULU
EKA	Mother earth	W AFRICAN
EKAEKA	To love very much	TSONGA
EKOKO	Continue a journey	XHOSA
EKUSENI	In the morning	ZULU
EKWINDLA	In autumn	ZULU
ELA	Flowing river	XHOSA
ELANA	To go somewhere for one another	TSONGA
ELEKELELI	Helper	ZULU
ELELA	To see clearly	TSONGA
ELEON	Beloved child of God	W AFRICAN
ELETSA	To wish or want	TSONGA
ELETSA	Advisor, thinker	TSONGA
ELHASILI	Finally, ultimately	SWAHILI
ELLA	To move towards	TSONGA

ELONA	The very one, the most	XHOSA
ELULEKI	Counselor, advisor	ZULU
EMA	Stand up and prepare to walk	SOTHO
EMARA	Conception	TSONGA
ENA	One's 'self'	ZULU
ENAMA	Be contented, happy	ZULU
ENANELA	Rejoice over	ZULU
ENDESHA	To go on, to guide	SWAHILI
ENEZEZELO	Addition	ZULU
ENGAMELI	President	ZULU
ENHLE	Beautiful	NGUNI
ENINGIZIMA	Of the south	ZULU
ENTLA	Of the north	XHOSA
ENTSHONALANGA	In the west	ZULU
ENYAKATHO	In the north	ZULU
ENYO	Enough children	W AFRICAN
ENZI	Majesty, sovereignty, power	SWAHILI
EREVU	Clever, shrewd	SWAHILI
ESASA	Be happy	ZULU
ESESE	In a secret place	ZULU
ESHE	Animated, spirited	W AFRICAN
ESI	Sunday's child, born on Sunday	W AFRICAN
ESONA	The very one, the most	XHOSA
ESUTHA	Satisfied with food	ZULU
ETANA	Robust and strong child	W AFRICAN
ETHABA	Be happy	ZULU
ETHEMBA	Trust, hope	ZULU
ETHEMBISO	Promise	ZULU

ETHUKA	Start	XHOSA
ETHUKA	Surprise	ZULU
ETHULO	Gift, present	ZULU
ETHUSA	Start	XHOSA
ETHWASA	Start anew	ZULU
ETSANE	Group of young people	TSONGA
EYONA	The very one, the best	XHOSA
EZE	King	W AFRICAN

FEZELA - SCORPION

FABAYO	A lucky birth that gives joy	W AFRICAN
FADHEELA	Excellence	ARABIC
FADHILI	Favor, kindness, grace	SWAHILI
FAFATSA	Light rain	S SOTHO
FAHAMU	Intellect, mind	SWAHILI
FAHLASI	Tall person	ZULU
FAIDA	Advantage	SWAHILI
FAIZA	Champion	ARABIC
FAKALLA	To have crooked legs	S SOTHO
FAKAZI	Jehovah's Witness	ZULU
FAKHARI	Excellence	SWAHILI
FANA	Resemble, likeness	XHOSA
FANANA	To resemble, likeness	SWAHILI
FANELA	Necessary	TSONGA
FANISA	Compare, imitate	TSONGA
FANISA	To resemble someone	ZULU
FARAA	Cheery, animated child	W AFRICAN
FARAJA	Comfort, rest	SWAHILI
FARASI	Horse	SWAHILI
FAREED	One of a kind – boy	ARABIC

FAREEDA	One of a kind – girl	ARABIC
FAREEHA	Joyful, happy	ARABIC
FARIDA	The only one – girl	ARABIC
FARIH	Light-complexioned	W AFRICAN
FARRAH	One who carries the burden	ARABIC
FATASHI	Provider	SWAHILI
FAYALO	Wealth and happiness	W AFRICAN
FAYEKA	Fragile	TSONGA
FAYOLA	Lucky	W AFRICAN
FAZI	A woman, a wife	XHOSA
FAZI	Womanhood	ZULU
FEDHA	Silver, money	SWAHILI
FEELI	Wonder, sign, omen	SWAHILI
FEFO	Storm, tempest	S SOTHO
FEMI	Child to be well loved, love me	W AFRICAN
FENENA	Persevere	S SOTHO
FENYA	Conquer, vanquish	S SOTHO
FERETA	Peace	S SOTHO
FERUZI	Turquoise	SWAHILI
FEZA	Complete, accomplish	XHOSA
FEZELA	Scorpion	NGUNI
FIKILE	She who has come	NGUNI
FIKILIZA	To fulfill	SWAHILI
FIKIRA	Thoughts, reflections	SWAHILI
FIKISA	Accompany to the end of the journey	TSONGA
FILA	Badness	SWAHILI
FINYELELA	To reach, to arrive	ZULU
FINYEZI	Firefly	ZULU
FIRYAL	Designation, epithet	ARABIC
FISHA	Short	ZULU

FOBELA	To gulp down, eat large mouthfuls	ZULU
FOKAZA	A great fellow	XHOSA
FOKAZI	Stranger	ZULU
FOLA	Glory and honor	W AFRICAN
FOPHISA	Pacifier	S SOTHO
FOWABO	His, her, their brother	ZULU
FOWENU	Your brother	ZULU
FREYA	Goddess of Love	SWAHILI
FUDU	Tortoise	ZULU
FUJO	She completes the family	E AFRICAN
FUKU	Deep water	TSONGA
FULA	Reap, gather crops from fields or river	ZULU
FUMA	To become rich	S SOTHO
FUMA	Reign, govern, command	TSONGA
FUMAHADI	Queen, princess, lady	S SOTHO
FUMBE	Riddle, puzzle	ZULU
FUMISA	Enrichment	TSONGA
FUMO	Lance, spear	SWAHILI
FUNANI	What are we searching for	ZULU
FUNDISA	Teach	ZULU
FUNDISWA	Learned person	XHOSA
FUNDZU	Tie a knot	TSONGA
FUNEKA	To be wanted, desirable	ZULU
FUPHI	Short, squat	XHOSA
FUPI	Short	SWAHILI
FUPUTSA	Think deeply	S SOTHO
FURAHA	Joy, gladness, pleasure	SWAHILI
FUSA	Dark brown	XHOSA
FUSI	Child born next after twins	ZULU
FUTHI	Again, once more	ZULU

FUTSA	To resemble, take after	S SOTHO
FUTSANA	To look alike	S SOTHO
FUVUKA	Try and try again	XHOSA
FUZA	Resemble, take after	ZULU
FUZO	Heredity, resemblance	ZULU

GAYA - BRANCH

GABA	To overflow or vain	XHOSA
GABADELI	He who acts with force	ZULU
GABADI	Earth	ZULU
GABHAZA	Travel freely and safely	XHOSA
GABISILE	She, who we can show off with	ZULU
GABUKA	Clearing of the mist	XHOSA
GABULA	Make a clearing or opening	XHOSA
GADA	To defend or protect	XHOSA
GADIMA	Lightning	SOTHO
GAGASI	Ocean wave	ZULU
GAGU	Expert at music, singing, dancing	ZULU
GAJELA	Tall, stout person	XHOSA
GAJULA	Walk through tall grass	XHOSA
GALA	Meerkat or ground squirrel	XHOSA
GAMA	Eagle	TSONGA
GAMA	Namesake	ZULU
GAMBA	Water tortoise	TSONGA
GANGI	Mischievous person	ZULU
GASA	Vain, conceited	XHOSA
GAUDA	Gold	S SOTHO

GAUTA	Golden	SOTHO
GAYA	Branch	NGUNI
GAZI	Strong personality	ZULU
GEDE	Honey guide	ZULU
GENDE	Queen of an ant community	XHOSA
GERDA	Snake charmer	W AFRICAN
GEZA	Handsome young man	ZULU
GHANIMA	Abundance, plenty, good fortune	SWAHILI
GHUBARI	Rain cloud	SWAHILI
GHUFIRA	Pardon, forgiveness	SWAHILI
GIBELI	Expert horseman	ZULU
GIDIMA	Run with speed	XHOSA
GIGITHA	Muse, daydream	XHOSA
GIJIMANI	A fast runner	ZULU
GIJIMI	Expert runner, messenger	ZULU
GITSHIMA	Messenger	XHOSA
GIYA	Victory dance	TSONGA
GOBUSETSA	Restoration	SOTHO
GODUKA	Prodigal son, return home	ZULU
GOEMELA	To represent someone, to take someone's place	SOTHO
GOIPOSELETSA	Revenge	N SOTHO
GOLEKANE	Enough, that will do	SOTHO
GOLOKA	To be righteous	SOTHO
GONANYA	Steady	N SOTHO
GONI	A promise	XHOSA
GONOTHI	Tall, slender person	ZULU
GONTSE	Enough	NGUNI
GORA	Brave and valiant man	XHOSA
GOSERESELO	To say nothing – to be silent	SOTHO
GOVA	Long narrow valley, gorge	TSONGA

GOVELA	Apprentice diviner	TSONGA
GOYA	Elegant gait	SWAHILI
GOYA	Wild cat	TSONGA
GOZI	An accident, misfortune	XHOSA
GRASIA	Grace	S SOTHO
GUGA	Strong and lasting	ZULU
GUGU	A jewel, treasure	XHOSA
GUKLU	Young pumpkin	ZULU
GULAI	Born between the rainy seasons	ZULU
GUMBA	White stork	TSONGA
GUZA	A secret	ZULU
GWADI	Pumpkin	TSONGA
GWAZI	Warrior who is an expert with a spear	ZULU
GWEBI	One who gives judgement	ZULU
GWEDI	Skillful carver, sculptor	ZULU
GWILI	Rich, prosperous person	ZULU

HAWU - SHIELD

HABIBA	Treasured daughter	E AFRICAN
HADITHI	Fable	SWAHILI
HADIYA	God's gift	N AFRICAN
HAKI	Justice	SWAHILI
HALEEMA	Calm, serene	ARABIC
HALIMA	Compassionate, kind, gentle	SWAHILI
HAMID	Prophet	ARABIC
HANAA	Happiness	SWAHILI
HANGWANI	Forget	VENDA
HANI	Joyful, happy	ARABIC
HASA	Special	SWAHILI
HASAN	Reliable, honorable	ARABIC
HASINA	First class, excellent, good	SWAHILI
HAWA	Eve, wife of Adam	ARABIC
HAWU	Shield	NGUNI
HAYA	Modesty	SWAHILI
HAYTHAM	Falcon	ARABIC
HAZIKA	Enlightened person, intelligent one	ARABIC
HERI	Happiness	SWAHILI

HESSA	Karma, fate	ARABIC
HIKIMA	Wisdom	SWAHILI
HIRIZI	Charm	SWAHILI
HISHIMA	Honor	SWAHILI
HLAGO	Nature	N SOTHO
HLANO	Five	N SOTHO
HLENGIWE	She has been protected	ZULU
HLOKOMILE	A loud person	NGUNI
HLOMPHO	Honor, respect	N SOTHO
HLONIPHILE	She has shown respect	ZULU
HLUPHEKILE	He struggles	ZULU
HONDO	Warrior, fighter	W AFRICAN
HURU	Free	SWAHILI
HURUMA	Compassion	SWAHILI
HUSANI	Handsome young man	SWAHILI
HUSANI	Handsome	SWAHILI

IMBUZI - CAT

IBADA	The adored one	SWAHILI
IBO	First fruits	XHOSA
IDI	Born during the Idi festival	SWAHILI
IDILI	Well behaved	SWAHILI
IFE	Love of art and culture	W AFRICAN
IFETAYO	Love brings happiness	W AFRICAN
IGE	Delivered feet first	C AFRICAN
IHAB	Blessing, gift	C ARABIC
IJARA	The reward	SWAHILI
IJUMAA	Friday	SWAHILI
IKETLA	Happy, carefree	S SOTHO
ILA	Birthmark	SWAHILI
ILA	Chaste, abstinence	SOTHO
ILOLA	To become strong	S SOTHO
IMAMU	Spiritual leader	W AFRICAN
IMANI	Faith	SWAHILI
IMARA	Strong, enduring	SWAHILI
IMBUZI	Cat	NGUNI
IMEN	Confidence, belief	ARABIC
IMOLA	Rescuer, to bring relief	S SOTHO

IMPELA	Truly	ZULU
INA	Placid and quiet, gentle, mother of the rains	C AFRICAN
INAM	He is with me	NGUNI
INAYA	Providence	SWAHILI
INATHI	God is with us	XHOSA
INDLA	Autumn	XHOSA
INKANTOLO	High rank	ZULU
INKOMU	We give thanks	TSONGA
INSHALLAH	If God is willing	SWAHILI
IROZI	Rose	ZULU
ISHARA	Miracle	SWAHILI
ISHI	Everlasting	SWAHILI
ISOKE	God blesses us with this child	W AFRICAN
ISRA	Journey of the night	ARABIC
ITA	The invited one	SWAHILI
IWELA	To struggle	SOTHO
IZEBE	Long-awaited child	W AFRICAN
IZIBULO	First-born	ZULU
IZOLO	Yesterday	ZULU

JEKAMANZI
DRAGONFLY

JABALANI	Happiness	NGUNI
JABARI	Courageous	W AFRICAN
JABBAR	Restorer – boy	ARABIC
JABEA	Gift from God	W AFRICAN
JABULANI	Come to bring happiness for everybody	N SOTHO
JAFAR	Flowing river	ARABIC
JAHA	Grandeur, majesty, dignity	NGUNI
JALALI	Majesty	SWAHILI
JAMAL	Beautiful, attractive	ARABIC
JAMEELA	Beautiful daughter	ARABIC
JAMILA	Elegant, lovely maiden	ARABIC
JANA	Yesterday	SWAHILI
JANAAN	Essence, incarnation	ARABIC
JANNA	Heaven	SWAHILI
JEKAMANZI	Dragonfly	NGUNI
JELA	Father suffered during birth of a son	W AFRICAN
JEMILA	Charming and delightful girl	E AFRICAN
JENDAYI	To give thanks for this child	W AFRICAN

JEROBA	The breaker	SOTHO
JINA	Name	SWAHILI
JIRANI	Neighbor	SWAHILI
JOJO	He who passes down stories	E AFRICAN
JOMO	Burning spear	KIKUYU
JONGILANGA	He faces the sun	NGUNI
JONGIWE	Look at me	XHOSA
JOZI	Couple, pair	SWAHILI
JUMOKE	Everyone loves this child	W AFRICAN
JUZA	Notify, announce	SWAHILI

KHOLWASI - FLAMINGO

KABELLO	Something shared	SOTHO
KABELO	Gift, beautiful share	SOTHO
KABISA	Entirely, completely	SWAHILI
KADIJA	Wife of Mohammed	W AFRICAN
KAFELE	Worthy of sacrifice	W AFRICAN
KAFI	Serene	SWAHILI
KAFIL	Protector, responsible	SWAHILI
KAGISO	Peace, let's build together	SOTHO
KAIDI	Stubborn	SWAHILI
KAINDA	The Provider's daughter, hunter's daughter	N AFRICAN
KALI	Sharp, fierce, energetic	SWAHILI
KALIFA	Child blessed by God	E AFRICAN
KAMALI	Ultimate fulfillment, perfection	W AFRICAN
KAMARIA	Bright as the moon, like the moon	ARABIC
KAMILI	Perfect	SWAHILI
KAMOGELO	An accepted child who was not planned	NGUNI

KANIKA	Dark covering, of the black cloth	ARABIC
KANONI	A type of small bird	SWAHILI
KARABO	Reply to my prayers	SOTHO
KARAMA	Gift	SWAHILI
KARIAMU	In the image of God	E AFRICAN
KARIBU	Near, close	SWAHILI
KASIKAZI	North	SWAHILI
KASUKU	Parrot	SWAHILI
KATI	Middle	SWAHILI
KATLEGO	Success	SOTHO
KATSE	Cat	N SOTHO
KAWERIA	Child who gives love, loving one	SWAHILI
KEITA	Devoted one	W AFRICAN
KELELE	Noisy	SWAHILI
KELINDE	Second-born twins	W AFRICAN
KENDA	Nine	SWAHILI
KESI	Born at a time of great trouble for the father	SWAHILI
KETHUKUTHULA	Choose to be silent	N SOTHO
KETO	Depth	SWAHILI
KEYAH	Blooming, flourishing, in good health	W AFRICAN
KGAITSEDI	Brother	ZULU
KGALEME	Gentle	NGUNI
KGANYA	To be bright, to shine	SOTHO
KGETHA	To choose	SOTHO
KGOSI	King	N SOTHO
KGOTHATSO	Console, pacify	N SOTHO
KGOTLA	A place where wise men gather	SOTHO

KGOTSO	Justice, peace	SOTHO
KGOTSOFALO	Satisfied	N SOTHO
KGWEBO	Wealth	SOTHO
KGWETE	The greatest, champion	SOTHO
KHADIJA	Child born prematurely	ARABIC
KHAIRIYA	Gracious, benevolent	ARABIC
KHALIDA	Eternal, everlasting	ARABIC
KHANGEZILE	Our hands are open	ZULU
KHANYISANI	Let there be light	NGUNI
KHANYISILE	Bright	ZULU
KHAYA	Home	ZULU
KHERI	Better	SWAHILI
KHOLWASI	Flamingo	NGUNI
KHUTSANA	Orphan	N SOTHO
KHUTSO	Peace, harmony	N SOTHO
KIAMBU	This one will be rich	E AFRICAN
KIANGA	Sunshine, sunbeams	C AFRICAN
KIBURI	Pride	SWAHILI
KILOLO	Youth shines upon her	SWAHILI
KINAH	Persistent	W AFRICAN
KIPAWA	Gift	SWAHILI
KISASI	Revenge	SWAHILI
KIVULI	Shadow	SWAHILI
KODJO	Monday's child	W AFRICAN
KOKAYI	Call the people to hear	N SOTHO
KOMBO	Crooked	SWAHILI
KOTSI	Accident	N SOTHO
KUBWA	Great	SWAHILI
KUFERE	Never forget	W AFRICAN
KUFIKA	To arrive	SWAHILI
KUHLE	It is beautiful	ZULU

KULEA	To nurse, to tend	SWAHILI
KUMETA	To shine, glow	SWAHILI
KUMI	Ten	SWAHILI
KURWA	Repeated	SWAHILI
KUSHIBA	To be satisfied	SWAHILI
KUSI	South	SWAHILI
KUTOSHA	Enough!	SWAHILI
KWACHA	In the morning	W AFRICAN
KWANELE	The last one (silent 'k')	ZULU
KWANZA	First	SWAHILI
KWELI	Truth	SWAHILI
KWENA	Crocodile	N SOTHO
KWESI	Overpowering strength	W AFRICAN
KWISISA	Listen very closely	SOTHO
KYUMBULANI	Remember	NGUNI

LANDA - EGRET

LABOBEDI	Tuesday	N SOTHO
LABOHLANO	Friday	SOTHO
LABONE	Thursday	N SOTHO
LABORARO	Wednesday	SOTHO
LAINI	Delicate	SWAHILI
LAMIA	Glitter	SWAHILI
LAMORENA	Sunday	N SOTHO
LANDA	Egret	NGUNI
LATEEFA	Tender, compassionate	ARABIC
LEBADI	Birthmark	SOTHO
LEBALA	Forget the lost child – I am here now	SOTHO
LEBITSO	Name	N SOTHO
LEBOGO	Thanksgiving	SOTHO
LEBONE	Candle, light	N SOTHO
LEBOPO	Deep place, valley	SOTHO
LEBOWA	North	N SOTHO
LEDIMO	Storm, tornado	SOTHO
LEEBANA	Bird	N SOTHO
LEENA	Compassionate, kind	ARABIC

LEFATSHE	Earth	N SOTHO
LEFOFA	Feather	N SOTHO
LEGADIMA	Flash of lightning	N SOTHO
LEGOBU	Chameleon	N SOTHO
LEGODIMO	Heaven	N SOTHO
LEGOTLO	Mouse	N SOTHO
LEHLABULA	Autumn	SOTHO
LEHLIMO	Luck, fortune	N SOTHO
LEHLOGONOLO	Blessing, prosperity	SOTHO
LEHUMO	Riches	N SOTHO
LEITSIBOLO	First-born, oldest child	N SOTHO
LEKANA	Equal	SOTHO
LEKANYA	To balance or equalize	SOTHO
LEKGAREBE	Lady, mistress	N SOTHO
LELA	Night	SWAHILI
LELAKABE	Flame	N SOTHO
LENGELOI	Angel	N SOTHO
LENONG	Eagle	N SOTHO
LEO	Today	SWAHILI
LERATADIMA	Clear skies	N SOTHO
LERATO	Love	N SOTHO
LEROLE	Dust storm	SOTHO
LERUBISHI	Owl	N SOTHO
LERUBISI	Owl	SOTHO
LERUMO	Blade – edge of a spear, cloud	N SOTHO
LESEDI	Clean, pure, bright, beautiful	N SOTHO
LESHATA	Loud noise	N SOTHO
LESOME	Ten	N SOTHO
LESWAO	Token	SOTHO
LETHABO	Happy, rejoicing	N SOTHO
LETLAPA	Rock	N SOTHO

LETSATSI	Day, sun	SOTHO
LETSHA	Lake	N SOTHO
LETSOBA	Beautiful flower	N SOTHO
LETSOBA	Dove, rose	N SOTHO
LETSOPA	Clay, earth	SOTHO
LEWATLE	Sea, large lake	SOTHO
LINA	Delicate, slight, tender	W AFRICAN
LINDELA	Wait for something	NGUNI
LINDIWE	We have waited patiently for this joy	NGUNI
LINDOKUHLE	Wait for the good	NGUNI
LISHA	Enigmatic, mystical, mysterious	W AFRICAN
LISIMBA	Undecided, wavering	W AFRICAN
LIYANDA	The nation is growing	NGUNI
LONDININGI	One who shelters and protects many people	NGUNI
LOYISO	Purity	NGUNI
LULAMA	Humble	NGUNI
LULU	Pearl	SWAHILI
LUMBWI	Chameleon	SWAHILI
LUMO	Born face-downwards	W AFRICAN
LUNGELWA	Things will work out well	NGUNI
LUNGILE	Friendly, someone who is faithful	ZULU

MABHENGWANE - OWL

MAARUFU	Celebrated	SWAHILI
MAATLA	Power	NGUNI
MABHENGWANE	Owl	NGUNI
MABOTSANA	Pretty woman	SOTHO
MABOTSE	Beautiful, bright	SOTHO
MABYOKO	Brain	ZULU
MACHUI	Like a leopard	SWAHILI
MADAHA	Elegant, charming	W AFRICAN
MADIBANA	Small river	SOTHO
MADIBENG	Among small rivers	SOTHO
MADIMABE	Bad luck	ZULU
MAEMO	Pride	N SOTHO
MAFUANE	Earthy, soil	C AFRICAN
MAFULO	Pasture	N SOTHO
MAGABARU	Greedy, voracious	N SOTHO
MAGANO	She is a gift from God	SWAHILI
MAHLATSE	Good luck, good fortune	SOTHO
MAHLATSI	Chance, luck, fortune	N SOTHO
MAHLIBE	Sunrise, dawn	N SOTHO
MAHLODI	Crane	SOTHO

MAHLOGONOLO	Good luck, popularity	N SOTHO
MAHLULI	Conqueror	W AFRICAN
MAHUMO	Riches, wealth	N SOTHO
MAISHA	Life	SWAHILI
MAJI	Water	SWAHILI
MAJIBU	Answer	SWAHILI
MAJONI	Soldier	XHOSA
MAKATSO	Wonder, astonishment	SOTHO
MAKENA	Cheerful daughter	W AFRICAN
MAKERUBU	Cherub	SWAHILI
MAKHA	Perfume	ZULU
MAKHULU	Grandmother	XHOSA
MAKINI	Placid	W AFRICAN
MAKJOSAZANE	Princess	NGUNI
MAKOTI	Daughter-in-law	N SOTHO
MALAIKA	Angel	SWAHILI
MALAK	Angel	ARABIC
MALEFI	He keeps traditions	NGUNI
MALENE	Pinnacle of strength	W AFRICAN
MALIKA	Princess	W AFRICAN
MALIZA	Riches	SWAHILI
MALKIA	Queen	SWAHILI
MAMBA	Crocodile	SWAHILI
MAMEPE	Honeycomb	SOTHO
MAMOYA	From the windy place	N SOTHO
MANDISA	Sweet milk, brandy	W AFRICAN
MANDLA	Power	NGUNI
MANDLA	Brave	ZULU
MANTUA	Daughter born during wartime	SOTHO
MANTWA	A lady who likes to fight	NGUNI
MAOBANE	Yesterday	N SOTHO

MAPEMA	Early	SWAHILI
MAPENZI	Love	SWAHILI
MAPHEFO	A child born on a windy day	NGUNI
MAPHELO	Well-being	SOTHO
MAPULA	Child born during the rains	SOTHO
MARATHI	Dew	SOTHO
MARATIWA	The favorite one	SOTHO
MAREGA	Winter	SOTHO
MARIAM	Fearless	ARABIC
MARIAMA	Gift from God	W AFRICAN
MARIGA	Winter	N SOTHO
MARIMBA	Mother of music, a musical instrument	NGUNI
MARIYAN	Brilliance, clarity	ARABIC
MARKA	Born during steady rains	W AFRICAN
MARU	Clouds	N SOTHO
MASHAMA	A surprise, unexpected	NGUNI
MASHUDU	Lucky	SOTHO
MASILO	Son of a beautiful daughter	SOTHO
MATATA	Trouble, tangle	SWAHILI
MATHAPAMA	Dawn	N SOTHO
MATHAPELO	Answer from God	NGUNI
MATHOMO	First-born	N SOTHO
MATILAI	East wind	SWAHILI
MATLA	Strength	SOTHO
MATLAKADIBE	Heavy rain	N SOTHO
MATLAKALA	One who sweeps the home clean	SOTHO
MATLAKGOGEDI	Grace, graceful	SOTHO
MATSATSI	A child born on a sunny day	NGUNI
MAUDUA	Spider's web	SOTHO
MAWINGU	Clouds	SWAHILI

MBALI	Flower, story	NGUNI
MBALI	Far away	SWAHILI
MBENGENI	Unknown	NGUNI
MBILI	Two	SWAHILI
MBIMBI	Cute	ZULU
MBINGU	Heaven	SWAHILI
MBONGENI	Let's thank him	NGUNI
MBUZENI	Ask him	NGUNI
MEBALA	The colorful one	SOTHO
MEDUPI	Silent rain	NGUNI
MEHLOLO	Mysterious	N SOTHO
MELUSI	Shepherd	NGUNI
MEMBATHISI	One who covers	NGUNI
MESO	Early	N SOTHO
MESONG	Morning	N SOTHO
METSI	Water	N SOTHO
METSIE	Water	SOTHO
MGENI	Traditions	SWAHILI
MILA	Stranger	SWAHILI
MINA	My 'self'	NGUNI
MJUMBE	Fierce	SWAHILI
MKALI	Messenger	SWAHILI
MKUKI	Spear	SWAHILI
MKWE	Daughter-in-law	SWAHILI
MLIMA	Mountain	SWAHILI
MMA	Mother's daughter	SOTHO
MMABALISA	Mother of Balisa	SOTHO
MMAKGOSI	Queen	SOTHO
MMALESATA	Woman of noise	SOTHO
MMAPULA	A girl born on a rainy day	NGUNI
MMUSI	Ruler, governor	N SOTHO

MMUTLA	Thorn	N SOTHO
MOAGISANI	Neighbor	N SOTHO
MODIRAKHUTSO	Peacemaker	N SOTHO
MODISIS	Shepherd, herdsman	N SOTHO
MODUMEDI	The believer	SOTHO
MOELETSI	Advisor, counselor	N SOTHO
MOETAPELE	Leader	N SOTHO
MOETAPELE	Leader	SOTHO
MOFENYI	Champion	N SOTHO
MOGHAWE	He who has not been conquered	ZULU
MOHAU	Mercy	SOTHO
MOHLOKOMEDI	Watchman, caretaker, protector	SOTHO
MOHLOLO	Miracle	N SOTHO
MOIAMO	Brother-in-law	N SOTHO
MOITHUTI	Scholar	N SOTHO
MOJA	One, single	SWAHILI
MOKIBELO	Saturday	N SOTHO
MOKITIMI	A fast runner, messenger	SOTHO
MOLAHLEGI	Abundance	N SOTHO
MOLALATLADI	Rainbow	N SOTHO
MOLALATLADI	Rainbow	SOTHO
MOLATSWANA	Small river	N SOTHO
MOLEMI	Farmer	N SOTHO
MOLLO	Fire	SOTHO
MOLWANTWA	An expert spearman, fighter	N SOTHO
MOMOHLA	Today	N SOTHO
MONAMEDI	Passenger	SOTHO
MONGO	Renowned, well known	W AFRICAN
MONOSI	Alone	N SOTHO
MONOSINOSI	Alone, only	N SOTHO
MONTSHO	Dark skinned	W AFRICAN

MONWABISI	The one who makes you happy	NGUNI
MOOFISIRI	Officer, captain	N SOTHO
MOOTLWA	Thorn	SOTHO
MOPOROFITA	Prophet	N SOTHO
MORANANG	April	N SOTHO
MORATUWA	The most loved one	SOTHO
MORITI	Shadow, messenger	N SOTHO
MORONGWA	Queen	W AFRICAN
MOROWA	Messenger	SOTHO
MORUTISI	Teacher	N SOTHO
MORWA	Son	N SOTHO
MORWA	Bushman, light-colored person	SOTHO
MORWANA	Bushman	N SOTHO
MOSADI	The planter of seed	SOTHO
MOSHATHAMA	Meaning unknown	NGUNI
MOSI	First-born twin	W AFRICAN
MOSIRELETSI	An opponent	N SOTHO
MOSUPULOGO	Monday	N SOTHO
MOTABOGI	A fast runner	N SOTHO
MOTAKI	Artist	SOTHO
MOTELELE	Tall and slender person	SOTHO
MOTHUSA	Benefactor, helper	SOTHO
MOTHUSI	Helper	SOTHO
MOTLALEPULA	Child that returns	N SOTHO
MOTO	Fire, heat	SWAHILI
MOTSADI	Guardian	N SOTHO
MOTSEGARE	Girl born at dawn	SOTHO
MOTSEMANE	A boy	SOTHO
MOTSESANE	A girl	SOTHO
MOTSHEGARE	Day	N SOTHO
MOTSUMI	Hunter	N SOTHO

MOTSWADI	She who gives life	SOTHO
MPHO	Gift	NGUNI
MPHONYANA	Gift, small present	N SOTHO
MPOLAYENG	A trouble maker	N SOTHO
MSHARE	Arrow	SWAHILI
MSIBA	Calamity	SWAHILI
MSICHANA	Damsel, maiden	SWAHILI
MTUNGA	Shepherd, herdsman	NGUNI
MUGABE	The weaponed attacker, slasher	SWAHILI
MUNIRA	Radiant	SWAHILI
MUUMBA	Creator	SHONA
MUWALI	Flame	SWAHILI
MVUA	Rain	SWAHILI
MWA	Blessing, grace	W AFRICAN
MWALUMI	The great teacher	SWAHILI
MWAMBA	Rock	SWAHILI
MWANA	Maiden	SWAHILI
MWARI	Son of a beautiful daughter	SWAHILI
MWENZI	Companion	SWAHILI
MWEZI	Moon	SWAHILI
MWIBA	Thorn	SWAHILI
MWISHO	Last one, end	SWAHILI
MWITA	He who announces	W AFRICAN
MWITI	Forest	SWAHILI
MWIZA	Beautiful	RUANDAN
MWIZA	One who forgives	SWAHILI
MXOLISA	Beautiful	XHOSA
MYEMYELA	Smile	RUANDAN
MZEE	Knowledgeable one, elder	SWAHILI
MZINGA	Cannon	SWAHILI
MZWANDILE	Noble	SWAHILI

NDLOVU - ELEPHANT

NABILA	The family has increased	SWAHILI
NAKUBUYA	Much-loved child	XHOSA
NALEDI	A star, eternal	ZULU
NALO	Beloved daughter	W AFRICAN
NAMEVA	Grace, mother of the earth	N SOTHO
NANA	Grace	W AFRICAN
NANDIPHA	You gave me	ZULU
NATASA	Skillful	XHOSA
NATHI	With us	SWAHILI
NAYLA	To gain, benefit	ZULU
NDEGI	Bird	SWAHILI
NDITSHENI	Leave me alone	SWAHILI
NDIWA	Dove	SWAHILI
NDLOVU	Elephant	NGUNI
NDUGU	Brother or sister, bounty	NGUNI
NEEMA	Grace	SWAHILI
NEO	Act of God, free gift	SWAHILI
NGAKA	A healer	N SOTHO
NGHAMULA	Rich man	N SOTHO
NGUVU	Power	SOTHO

NGWANA	Child born during the rains	SOTHO
NGWEDI	Moon	N SOTHO
NHLANHLA	Luck	ZULU
NINI	Solid as a rock	W AFRICAN
NKASAZANA	Princess	ZULU
NKASINATHI	God is with us	ZULU
NKO	Nose	NGUNI
NKOSANA	Oldest child	ZULU
NKRUMAH	Ninth-born	W AFRICAN
NNETI	Truth	SOTHO
NOBANTU	Will be loved by everyone	NGUNI
NOBUHLE	Gorgeous child	NGUNI
NOCAEWE	She was born on Sunday	ZULU
NOKA	River	ZULU
NOKHWEZI	Morning star	NGUNI
NOKUPHELA	Love	SOTHO
NOKUUNJA	Abundance	XHOSA
NOKWANDA	Happiness	N SOTHO
NOLUTHANDO	Destiny, fate	ZULU
NOLWAZI	Knowledge	XHOSA
NOMASONTO	Born on Sunday	ZULU
NOMAWETHU	Ours	NGUNI
NOMBULELO	I give thanks	ZULU
NOMGXEBELO	Born on Saturday	ZULU
NOMONDE	Dedicated, patient	NGUNI
NOMOYA	From the windy place	XHOSA
NOMPUMELELO	Mother of success	ZULU
NOMSA	Kindness is found	ZULU
NOMTHANDAZO	We pray to the ancestors	NGUNI
NOMUSA	This is mercy	NGUNI
NOMVULA	She who brings the rains	NGUNI

NONHLANHLA	Daughter of luck	NGUNI
NONI	Blessing from God	W AFRICAN
NONTANDO	Full of love	NGUNI
NONYANA	Bird	SOTHO
NONZENSELE	She will do it herself	NGUNI
NOSI	Alone, only	NGUNI
NOTAGI	Sweet milk, brandy	SOTHO
NOZIPHO	This child is a gift	NGUNI
NOZIZWE	Mother of nations	NGUNI
NTANDAZO	Someone who prays	XHOSA
NTHABANG	Make us happy	SOTHO
NTOKOZO	Joy	SOTHO
NTSEBENG	Know me	SWAZI
NTWA	War	SOTHO
NTWASAHLOBO	Autumn	ZULU
NUNGU	Porcupine	N SOTHO
NUSU	Half	ZULU
NYIKA	Desert, wilderness	SWAHILI
NYONGA	Feather	SWAHILI

O

ONI - BIRD

OBAKHO	Yours	ZULU
OBALA	Out in the open, clearly	ZULU
OBAMI	This is mine	ZULU
OBENU	Yours	ZULU
OBETHU	Ours	ZULU
OCHI	Merriment and joy	W AFRICAN
ODION	First-born twin	W AFRICAN
ODWA	The only one	XHOSA
OGBO	Friend, mate, twin	W AFRICAN
OJI	Bearer of gifts	SWAHILI
OKOKA	To be saved	SWAHILI
OKON	Born after sunset	W AFRICAN
OKONA	The best, the nicest	XHOSA
OKUHLE	May you have good luck	ZULU
OKUMHLOPHE	Good luck to you	ZULU
OKWAM	My own	XHOSA
OKWAMI	Mine	ZULU
OKWENU	Yours	ZULU
OKWETHU	Ours	ZULU
OLABISI	Joy is multiplied	SWAHILI

OLONA	The most	XHOSA
OLOVA	Good hearted	TSONGA
OLUFEMI	Beloved daughter of God	W AFRICAN
OLUFUNKE	God-given child	W AFRICAN
OLULA	Stretched, drawn out	XHOSA
OLUREMI	God brings me comfort	W AFRICAN
OLWETHU	Our child	XHOSA
OMBA	To pray for, to beseech	SWAHILI
OMBELA	Sing to a beat, drumbeat	XHOSA
OMELA	Delicate	SOTHO
OMOLARA	Much-wanted child	W AFRICAN
ONALENNA	He or she is with me	SOTHO
ONDLEKA	Healthy, to be well cared for	ZULU
ONGA	To be saved	ZULU
ONGAMA	To stand out, to tower over	XHOSA
ONGEZA	To increase the numbers	ZULU
ONI	Bird	NGUNI
ONWABA	To be contented, satisfied	XHOSA
OSEGYEFO	Savior of the people	W AFRICAN
OSUJI	Farmer	W AFRICAN
OTHA	A name for the sun	XHOSA
OTHAMELA	To bask in the sun	ZULU
OTHULA	To give a gift in thanks	ZULU
OTHUSA	To be startled, surprised	XHOSA
OWENU	Yours	ZULU
OWETHU	Ours	ZULU
OWONA	The most, the best	XHOSA
OYA	A small handful	SWAHILI

PHEMPETHWANE
COBRA

PAA	Gazelle	SWAHILI
PABALLO	Favor, grace	SOTHO
PAKA	Cat	SWAHILI
PAKI	Observer, one who watches	W AFRICAN
PAMBO	Adornment	SWAHILI
PANYA	Mouse	SWAHILI
PANYAZA	An attractive girl with large eyes	ZULU
PARA	A pair	SOTHO
PATA	Twin	SWAHILI
PEKEE	Alone	SWAHILI
PEKETU	To reveal a secret	ZULU
PELONOMI	Patience	N SOTHO
PENDA	Love	SWAHILI
PEYAKANYO	Contrary	SOTHO
PHAHLA	One of twins	ZULU
PHAKAMILE	She who is on top of things	NGUNI
PHAKATHI	In the middle, between others	ZULU
PHAMBI	In front of, in the lead	ZULU
PHANDLA	To dazzle	ZULU

PHAPHAMA	To awaken	ZULU
PHAPHAZI	Butterfly	ZULU
PHATSHIMO	Shine brightly	N SOTHO
PHAZI	As a flash of lightning	ZULU
PHEETSO	Finish	N SOTHO
PHEIJANA	Youngest child, last-born	SOTHO
PHELETSO	Entirely, completely	N SOTHO
PHEMPETHWANE	Cobra	NGUNI
PHEPHELO	A haven, a shelter	ZULU
PHETHELA	To reach the end	ZULU
PHETHO	Complete	N SOTHO
PHETOLO	Answer	N SOTHO
PHEZULU	The heavens	ZULU
PHIKELELI	A patient person	ZULU
PHILA	To be healthy and strong	ZULU
PHINDILE	Again	NGUNI
PHISO	Fire, heat	N SOTHO
PHOFUKAZI	A woman with a fair complexion	ZULU
PHOOKA	Dew	N SOTHO
PHOPHOMA	A waterfall	ZULU
PHOTOKO	Gift	XHOSA
PHUMELELE	Succeeded	NGUNI
PHUMEZA	Success	XHOSA
PHUMLA	Now we can rest	NGUNI
PHUMZILE	She who made us rest	ZULU
PHUNYU	Breaking free from restrictions, liberating	ZULU
PINA	Song	N SOTHO
PINGU	Charm	SWAHILI
POELANO	Reconciled	N SOTHO
POMBOO	Porpoise	SWAHILI

POPO	Butterfly	SWAHILI
POTINGANA	Baby	ZULU
POTSISO	Question	N SOTHO
POTSO	Ask	N SOTHO
PULA	Rain	N SOTHO
PULENG	Child born in the rain	SOTHO
PUSELETSO	Child who replaces another	N SOTHO

Q
QHIMILILI
GECKO

QABAZA	Falling of large raindrops when it starts to rain	ZULU
QALELA	To start in good time	ZULU
QALELELA	To make an early start	ZULU
QAMATA	Great spirit	XHOSA
QAMBI	An inventor or composer	ZULU
QAPHELI	Someone who watches	ZULU
QEKETHA	To chatter incessantly	ZULU
QHABA	Falling raindrops	ZULU
QHAKAZA	To bloom or shine brightly	ZULU
QHAMA	To stand out among others	ZULU
QHANAGO	A feeling of pride	ZULU
QHAWE	Hero	ZULU
QHEZEBA	Strong, well-built person	ZULU
QHIMILILI	Gecko	NGUNI

RAFIKI - FRIEND

RAADI	Thunder	SWAHILI
RABAB	Soft clouds	ARABIC
RABABI	Silver	SWAHILI
RABIA	Spring	ARABIC
RADHI	Satisfied, contented	SWAHILI
RAFIKI	Friend	SWAHILI
RAHEEDA	Sagacious, discerning	ARABIC
RAHIDA	Honorable, moral	W AFRICAN
RAHISI	Easy	SWAHILI
RAI	Strength, prudence	SWAHILI
RAISA	President	SWAHILI
RAJA	Dreams and desires	ARABIC
RAMLA	Divination	SWAHILI
RANA	Watch over, wonder	ARABIC
RANGA	Of many colors	XHOSA
RANYA	To observe, to look upon	ARABIC
RAPULA	Father of rain	N SOTHO
RAPULANE	Father of soft rain	N SOTHO
RASHA	Gazelle	ARABIC
RATYA	Dusk, twilight	XHOSA

RAYA	Quenched a thirst	ARABIC
RAZIYA	Amiable	W AFRICAN
REEMA	Pale complexion	ARABIC
REFU	Tall, long	SWAHILI
REHEMA	Sensitive and understanding	W AFRICAN
RENDZO	A journey or pilgrimage	TSONGA
RHANDZA	Love	TSONGA
RHANGELA	The first one, to lead the way	TSONGA
RHUMBUKA	Blossom, flower	TSONGA
RIFUMU	Riches, wealth	TSONGA
RIKA	An equal	SWAHILI
RIKHOZI	Eagle	TSONGA
RIMPFANI	Chameleon	TSONGA
RIRHANDZU	Charity, love, goodwill	TSONGA
RISANA	A small boy, ray of sunlight	TSONGA
RIWA	A pasture or meadow	XHOSA
ROBANG	A harvest	SOTHO
ROHO	Spirit of life, soul	SWAHILI
ROLIHLOHLA	The one who opens the way	XHOSA
RUAZA	First of its kind, a model	SWAHILI
RUBANI	A guide	SWAHILI
RUFARO	Exuberance and joy	W AFRICAN

SIMBA - LION

SAADA	Helping hand, guide	W AFRICAN
SAALIMA	Guarded against harm	ARABIC
SABA	Seven	SWAHILI
SABRA	Patience	SWAHILI
SAHAR	Sunrise, dawn	ARABIC
SAHARA	The great and beautiful desert of Africa	ARABIC
SAHLA	Velvety, sleek	ARABIC
SAKEENA	Peace granted by God	ARABIC
SAKILE	Peace and beauty	NGUNI
SALAMA	Safety, peace, well-being	SWAHILI
SALIMA	Safe	SWAHILI
SALMA	Tranquil, quiet	ARABIC
SAMAWI	Blue	SWAHILI
SAMEERA	Amusing friend	ARABIC
SAMIRA	Reconciler	SWAHILI
SANA	Dazzling, radiant	ARABIC
SANI	An accident	SWAHILI
SANYA	Shining, bright	ARABIC
SAUDA	Black, dark complexion	SWAHILI

SEBEREKI	The worker	SOTHO
SEENYWA	Fruit	N SOTHO
SEFEFO	Storm	N SOTHO
SEGOKGO	Spider	SOTHO
SEKANI	Merriment and joy	W AFRICAN
SEKGWA	Forest	N SOTHO
SEKLARE	Three	N SOTHO
SELEMO	Summer	N SOTHO
SELEMO	Springtime	SOTHO
SELLO	A child who cries a lot	SOTHO
SELPATI	One who hides away	SOTHO
SEMAKALENG	Don't wander	NGUNI
SENEME	We are happy	ZULU
SENYANE	Nine	N SOTHO
SENZELWE	It has been done for us	ZULU
SEOKGO	Spider	N SOTHO
SEPHIRI	Secret	N SOTHO
SERIPA	Half	N SOTHO
SERITHI	Dignified	N SOTHO
SERURUBELE	Springbuck, butterfly	N SOTHO
SERUTHWANA	Spring	SOTHO
SESI	Sister	SOTHO
SESOLO	For nothing, free	N SOTHO
SESWAI	Eight	N SOTHO
SEWELA	Daughter of a beautiful son	SOTHO
SHAADIYA	Singer	ARABIC
SHAKA	Stomach disorder	ZULU
SHAKILA	Well shaped	SWAHILI
SHANI	Amazing child	W AFRICAN
SHAREEFA	Imposing, impressive	ARABIC
SHEMEGI	Brother-in-law	SWAHILI

SHIBA	Abundance	SWAHILI
SHIDA	With difficulty	SWAHILI
SHINDA	Excel	SWAHILI
SHUARI	Calm, placid	SWAHILI
SHUJAA	Warrior	SWAHILI
SHUWARI	Calm, placid	SWAHILI
SIAFU	Ant	SWAHILI
SIALA	Question	SWAHILI
SIBONGILE	Thanks	ZULU
SIBUSISO	Blessing	NGUNI
SIFA	Fame, praise	SWAHILI
SIHLE	Beautiful	NGUNI
SIKU	Day	SWAHILI
SIMBA	Lion	SWAHILI
SIPHINDILE	Another baby	XHOSA
SIPHO	A great gift	NGUNI
SIPHOKAZI	Gift	NGUNI
SIRI	Secret	SWAHILI
SITA	Six	SWAHILI
SITHABILE	We are happy	NGUNI
SIZWE	Nation	NGUNI
SOMO	Chum, pal	SWAHILI
SONTAGA	Sunday	SOTHO
SONTAHA	Sunday	SOTHO
SUBIRA	Patience	SWAHILI
SUHAYLA	Serene, tranquil	ARABIC
SULE	He who takes chances	W AFRICAN
SURAYYA	Noble	SWAHILI
SURIA	Concubine	SWAHILI

THETHE GRASSHOPPER

TAABU	Difficulty	SWAHILI
TAAHIRA	Innocent, virtuous	ARABIC
TAANISA	Sociable	SWAHILI
TABIA	Well-behaved girl	W AFRICAN
TAFIDA	Benefit	SWAHILI
TAI	Eagle	SWAHILI
TAIWO	First-born twin	W AFRICAN
TAJI	Crown	SWAHILI
TAKALANI	Happiness, happy	VENDA
TAKATIFU	Sacred	SWAHILI
TALI	Lion	N SOTHO
TAMAA	Desire, ambition	SWAHILI
TAMU	Sweet	SWAHILI
TANO	Five	SWAHILI
TATO	Three	SWAHILI
TAWIA	First-born twin	W AFRICAN
TAYMURA	Guardian	SWAHILI
TEBALO	Forget	N SOTHO
TEBOGO	Thanks, gratitude	SOTHO
TEKANO	Equal	N SOTHO

TEKENE	Sign	SOTHO
TELENA	Smooth, slippery	C AFRICAN
THABA	Mountain	N SOTHO
THABANG	Come to bring happiness	N SOTHO
THABANG	Come to bring happiness to everyone, be glad	SOTHO
THABO	Happy	SOTHO
THANAA	Gratitude	ARABIC
THANDEKA	Lovable	NGUNI
THANDEKILE	She who is very lovable	NGUNI
THANDI	Lovable	NGUNI
THANDISWA	She who had to be loved	ZULU
THANDIWE	Loved one	NGUNI
THANDO	Love	ZULU
THAPELO	Prayer	NGUNI
THATO	Having the will to achieve, determined to succeed	SOTHO
THAWABU	Reward	SWAHILI
THEMA	Queen	C AFRICAN
THEMBA	One who can be trusted, trustworthy	NGUNI
THEMBA	Hope	ZULU
THEMBEKILE	The trustworthy one	ZULU
THEMBI	To trust – female	NGUNI
THEMBILE	We trust in you	XHOSA
THETHE	Grasshopper	NGUNI
THOBELA	Obey	XHOSA
THOKOZILE	Happiness	NGUNI
THORAYA	Star	ARABIC
THOZAMA	Be quiet	XHOSA
THULANI	Humble, quiet	ZULU

THUMUNI	Eighth	SWAHILI
THURAYA	Star	ARABIC
THUTIWA	Giraffe	N SOTHO
TIBIMALO	Humble, quiet	N SOTHO
TIISETSO	Perseverance	SOTHO
TISA	Nine	SWAHILI
TLEKA	To clean up, to purify	SOTHO
TLOKOMELA	Caring for someone	SOTHO
TLOMPHA	Respect	SOTHO
TLORISO	To torment, to torture	SOTHO
TLOWANA	Little elephant	SOTHO
TOKO	Kind, good	N SOTHO
TOKOLOGO	Free	N SOTHO
TORKWASE	Queen	W AFRICAN
TOTO	Baby	SWAHILI
TSHEGOFATSO	Blessed	NGUNI
TSHELELA	Six	N SOTHO
TSHEPISO	Promise	N SOTHO
TSHEPO	Endeavor, hope, trust	N SOTHO
TSHIAMO	Enough!, honest	N SOTHO
TSHOKOLO	He struggles	N SOTHO
TSHOTSHWANE	Ant	N SOTHO
TSHOVHONALA	It will show	NGUNI
TSHWAETSO	Affection	N SOTHO
TSHWARELANO	Reconciled, forgiveness	SOTHO
TSHWARELO	Forgiveness	N SOTHO
TSHWELELO	Prosperous	SOTHO
TULINAGWE	God is with us	C AFRICAN
TUMA	Immortal	SOTHO
TUMAINI	Hope	SWAHILI
TUMELO	Believe	N SOTHO

TUMILE	The one who is famous	SOTHO
TUMISO	Praise to God	SOTHO
TUMPE	Let us thank God for this blessing	C AFRICAN
TUNDA	Fruit	SWAHILI
TUNU	A new thing, something new	SWAHILI
TWIGA	Giraffe	SWAHILI

U

UFUDO - TORTOISE

UBONGO	Brain	SWAHILI
UBORO	Powerful and superior	SWAHILI
UCHAO	Dawn, sunrise	SWAHILI
UDOGO	Youthfulness	SWAHILI
UDONGO	Earth	SWAHILI
UFANIFU	Success and prosperity	SWAHILI
UFUDO	Tortoise	NGUNI
UHURU	Freedom	SWAHILI
UKUU	Greatness, strength	SWAHILI
ULINZI	The watchman	SWAHILI
ULIZA	To question	SWAHILI
ULWESINE	Thursday	ZULU
UMBU	Sister	SWAHILI
UMDENI	Growing family	ZULU
UMEME	Lightning	SWAHILI
UMI	My mother	SWAHILI
UMKHONTSO	Blessed	NGUNI
UMZALI	Guardian	ZULU
UNGI	Plentiful, to have a multitude	SWAHILI
UNWANA	Another one	TSONGA

UNWE	The only one, unique	TSONGA
UPAJI	Gift	SWAHILI
UPENZI	Lovingness	SWAHILI
UPOLE	Gentleness	SWAHILI
UPYA	Something new	SWAHILI
URBI	Princess	W AFRICAN
UREFU	To be tall, tallness	SWAHILI
USAFI	Purity	SWAHILI
USHUJAA	Courage	SWAHILI
USIKU	Night	SWAHILI
USOMO	Fellowship	SWAHILI
UTAJIRI	Riches, wealth	SWAHILI
UTUKUFU	Glory	SWAHILI
UTULIZI	One who brings comfort	SWAHILI
UZIMA	Health, well-being	SWAHILI
UZIWA	To be deep, open sea	SWAHILI
UZUNGO	The halo around the moon	SWAHILI
UZURI	Beauty	SWAHILI

VUZIMANZI WATER SNAKE

VAKASA	To roam or meander, nomad	XHOSA
VANGA	To mingle well	XHOSA
VANGAMA	Dazzling, brilliant	TSONGA
VARASHA	A sentinel, a watchman	XHOSA
VATI	Birthmark	TSONGA
VEGA	Shooting star	ARABIC
VELA	Prominent one, to be taller	ZULU
VEMVANE	Butterfly	ZULU
VIKELI	Protector	ZULU
VINDZUKA	One who starts early in the morning	TSONGA
VITA	War	SWAHILI
VIZURI	Beautiful, pretty	SWAHILI
VUKANA	A young bull	ZULU
VUKOSI	Power, opulence	TSONGA
VULA	Rain	ZULU
VULINDABA	The beginning of the story	SOTHO
VUMBILU	Patience and goodness	TSONGA
VUMELA	In harmony with	ZULU
VUNA	To reap, to harvest	SWAHILI

VUNENE	Graciousness, virtue	TSONGA
VUNGUZA	A strong wind	ZULU
VUSA	To awaken	ZULU
VUSIMUZI	What am I saying	VENDA
VUTHA	Blazing, ardent, glowing	XHOSA
VUYA	Delighted, rejoicing	XHOSA
VUYELWA	Child that brings great joy	XHOSA
VUYISWA	Child that makes us happy	ZULU
VUZIMANZI	Water snake	NGUNI

WABAYI - RAVEN

WABAYI	Raven	NGUNI
WAGAO	Yours	N SOTHO
WAKUFU	Dedicated, sacred	SWAHILI
WALOWO	Each and every one	XHOSA
WANDILE	Growing family	NGUNI
WARDA	Rose	W AFRICAN
WARONA	Ours	N SOTHO
WAZA	One who reflects	SWAHILI
WEDWA	Only you, thou alone	XHOSA
WELILE	We have crossed over	ZULU
WENA	You	SOTHO
WIMBI	Wave	SWAHILI
WINA	A successful person	ZULU
WINGU	Cloud	SWAHILI
WOKOFU	Salvation, deliverance	SWAHILI
WOLOLA	One who cries all the time	ZULU
WOLOLO	One who cries all the time	ZULU
WONGA	A handsome figure	XHOSA
WONYO	A deep place, ravine, chasm	XHOSA
WOWU	One who is a pleasant surprise	ZULU

XOXO - FROG

XAVERIE	Bright light	ARABIC
XELA	Having a great resemblance	XHOSA
XOLANI	Forgive	NGUNI
XOLELWA	A child of peace	XHOSA
XOLILE	We have forgiven	ZULU
XOXO	Frog	NGUNI

YABA - FLOCK

YABA	Flock	NGUNI
YAKINI	Truth, honesty	SWAHILI
YANTAZA	To ramble about	XHOSA
YATIMA	Orphan	SWAHILI
YAZALALA	One who smoothes out, makes even	XHOSA
YEDWA	He alone, the only one	XHOSA
YNUGI	Water lily	SWAHILI
YOKO	The best of all, abundance of all good things	XHOSA
YOLA	Delightful, agreeable	XHOSA
YUSRA	Child born with ease	SWAHILI

ZIBU - WATER LILY

ZAAFIRA	Triumphant	ARABIC
ZAFARANI	Saffron	SWAHILI
ZAHARA	From the desert	ARABIC
ZAHIRA	Glittering	ARABIC
ZAHRA	Beautiful flower	SWAHILI
ZAHRAH	Beautiful flower	ARABIC
ZAIDEE	Blooming, flourishing	ARABIC
ZAINA	Beautiful daughter	ARABIC
ZAKIYA	Discerning and bright, intelligent	ARABIC
ZALANA	One who is related by blood, a relative	ZULU
ZALBAK	Mercury, quicksilver	SWAHILI
ZALIKA	An easy birth, wellborn	C AFRICAN
ZAMU	To watch	SWAHILI
ZANDILE	They have increased	SOTHO
ZANELE	Enough children	NGUNI
ZANI	Accident	SWAHILI
ZARA, ZAHRA	White bloom	ARABIC
ZERA	Beauty, blossoms at dawn	SWAHILI

ZIBA	A deep pool in a river	XHOSA
ZIBU	Water lily	ZULU
ZIKA	To understand thoroughly, to get to the bottom of	XHOSA
ZIMA	Whole, complete, healthy	SWAHILI
ZIMELA	One who hides away	XHOSA
ZINA	Beauty	SWAHILI
ZINDLA	One who ponders	XHOSA
ZINGIRA	To comfort	SWAHILI
ZINTLE	Beautiful girl	NGUNI
ZINZA	One who is firmly settled	XHOSA
ZINZI	Comfortably settled	XHOSA
ZIWA	Pond or lake	SWAHILI
ZOLA	Humble, quiet	ZULU
ZOLEKA	The meek one	XHOSA
ZOLO	Dew	ZULU
ZONDA	One who is doted upon, loved greatly	XHOSA
ZONGILE	Preserved	ZULU
ZOTHA	One who has dignity and self-possession	ZULU
ZOTHE	Steadfast, to stand like a rock	XHOSA
ZOTSHOLO	An expert, a skilled person	XHOSA
ZUBAYDA	The best one	SWAHILI
ZUKA	To come onto the scene as an upstart	SWAHILI
ZUKA	Famous, renowned, someone who is honored	XHOSA
ZUKISA	Be patient	XHOSA
ZULA	To roam about, to wander	ZULU

ZULU	A member of the Zulu race, or lightning	ZULU
ZUMA	One sneaking about at night with bad intent	XHOSA
ZUNA	Opulence, abundance and riches	C AFRICAN
ZURI	Handsome or beautiful	SWAHILI
ZUZA	Rewards and profits	XHOSA